LIVE FREE AND FOREVER

KENNETH FENLEY, JR.

Live Free and Forever

Copyright © 2018 by Kenneth Fenley, Jr.
Published by: Full Bloom Publishing

All rights reserved. In accordance with the U.S. Copyright Act of 1976, no part of this publication may be reproduced in any form or by any means, including scanning, photocopying, or otherwise without prior written permission from the copyright holder.

ISBN : **13: 978-0-9852839-6-4**

Published in the United States of America

Language: English

Dedication

This book is dedicated to my 4 wonderful children, Tierra, Taylor, Corey and Kennedi. As I push you, I push me! May my sacrifice be a seed for your success! Live free and forever!!

-Dad

Table of Contents

Chapter 1: The Gift

Chapter 2: Know Your Box

Chapter 3: "F" Is For Failure

Chapter 4: You Only Get An "E" For Effort.... That's All

Chapter 5: You Can Get An "A" If You Go All The Way

Chapter 6: Are You Gone Talk or Walk It Out

Chapter 1
The Gift

Growing up as a child, my favorite time of the year was Christmas!! I loved the idea of getting new things and couldn't wait to see if Santa (Mom and Dad) was going to get me exactly what I asked for. To wake up every morning during the month of December and see new presents under the tree gave me hope that maybe, just maybe, this would be the year I would get what I wanted. There was five of us in the house, so I would have to go through every box to see which one of them had my name on it. Each time I went to the tree, I would map my route (in my head) to the gifts I wanted to unwrap first. Then I would begin to section them off (you know, keep them away from everybody else's gift) to make sure there was no confusion on what was mine and theirs. It felt good knowing how many I had and where they were every night before I went to sleep.

Now my parents would make sure that every gift was wrapped and in a box. No matter if it was socks, underwear, clothes, whatever, they made sure it was in a box gift wrapped.

I now know as an adult with children, the only pleasure you get out of the holiday is watching your kids tear the paper off as they are in search of the hidden treasure. Sometimes my parents would go the extra mile and pick different wrapping paper for each child. For example, one year they did fruit and I was an apple or grape or.... well I really don't remember, but I know I received a really cool video game that year. Regardless of the paper, I would only open my gifts based on the size and weight of the box anyway. If it was big and heavy, then I would open it first. If it was small and light, then it was probably the pack of socks and underwear my grandmother got me and there was no need to be in a rush to open those, I already knew what it was. I was so intrigued to see if my parents were listening and actually got the thing I wanted that I raced to the tree with no hesitation. More times than not, they weren't able to and just got me what they could afford but that's another story for another day.

It was our tradition to open our presents at midnight Christmas Day. We spent the whole Christmas Eve begging our parents to open them sooner to no avail. As I would pick up every gift and unwrap it, my excitement and appreciation for the holiday would grow. If you are like me, then you just ripped the paper off with no regards for the time it took your parents to wrap it or amount of money they spent on the paper itself. I had one goal in mind, get to what was inside the box by any means necessary! But looking back I realize that some of my best gifts actually came in small packages. You see it was never about the box, it was about what the box contained. After it was all said and done, there would be a pile of paper and boxes set to the side leaving each child to hold on to what was inside the box. Looking back at those times, I realized a few things about boxes:

- **Boxes are designed to store things.**
  True enough, the bigger the item, the bigger the box and sometimes, bigger boxes are used based on the value of the item. But the box itself has very little value. And if there was nothing to contain, then the box would have no value at all.

- **Boxes are used during transition.**
  The movement of material will always be needed, especially if you want to protect what you're transporting. So, to get product from one place to another, the manufacturer places the items in a box to ensure what was being carried could not be damaged.

- **Boxes are used for hiding things.**
  The unknown creates an expectation. And that's even greater if a picture of the item is on the outside of the box. But no matter what the size, length, width or weight of the gift was, we were never able to see what was inside the box until the box was opened.

What does that have to do with you? Much like my Christmas experience, you are the gift that other people are waiting for. You were created for a purpose. For far too long you have lived your life stored inside of a box. To be stored, simply means to be put aside for a future use. So, maybe you have found yourself sitting in a room, staring at the walls and doing nothing with your potential. Or sitting at a desk or in a cubicle waiting on your moment to finally get here. Maybe you have been working in a warehouse and you are full of ideas and talent but inside you feel like now is not a good time. That's a clear indication that you have been stored up waiting for the right moment and conditions just to unleash the very thing you were created to do. But I want to tell you that greatness doesn't wait. It doesn't ask for permission. It's not standing on the outside of a double-dutch line waiting patiently to jump in. It seizes every moment. It maximizes every opportunity. Because it knows, there's no better time than this for me to do what I was created to do!!!

Now, transition is probably the most difficult part of life. It involves making a decision that where you are now, is no longer where you want to be. With that in mind, you have to fix your eyes on a target and move to land dead center on your mark. This should create a burning desire to get to a place where you can be all you were created to be. My favorite gift was that video game that I had begged for months. But the video game by itself is nothing until it fulfills its purpose. It had to be moved from the place of conception, relocate to a store, and then purchased, brought home, unwrapped, opened, just to be placed inside the gaming console to be played. Only after going through every phase, had the ultimate purpose of the game been fulfilled.

Most people give up after realizing they have to relocate more than once. Don't you dare let yourself become discouraged along the journey. Go ahead and get in your head now, you cannot stay where you are now. And you are going to have to move on from your next place as well. Yep, that's right!! You are going to have to continue to move on from each place of your life until you reach your full potential. You can't stop at the place of hurt or disappointment. You're going to have to move on past heart break and sorrow. And as much as you enjoy being happy and at peace, those places bring a false since of accomplishment, so yeah, you need to move on past those places as well. The key is to never become complacent. Remember you move in plateaus. You go up and then you even out. You step higher and then you learn to live on that level. But that step was not your last. It was just an indication that there was more in you. And every step after that, to reach your next level, you're going to have to put in more work than you have ever done to get there.

Finally, to be hidden doesn't feel good but it is not always a bad thing. Some things need to be hidden until they fully mature. Releasing your potential too soon could actually do more harm than good. There is a process that you must go through. It is the evolution of you becoming everything you were created to be. Think about a cake. When making a cake, the oven is closed until the appropriate time. It remains hidden as it goes through the process of becoming a cake. If you take it out too soon, you run the risk of losing the time and effort you put into making the cake. Eating the cake beforehand will leave you sick to the stomach. Either way, if the cake is not hidden long enough to fully go through the process, it can never become what it was intended to be.

You may feel as if you have been hidden your whole life. But there is a set time for revealing. There is a season for everything. A time when all things come together to make a treat that is good enough for the world to eat of. There is a time when everything you have faced in your life time begins to make since. Now that doesn't change the past experiences and it may not even take away the sting from the pain, but to know that you have survived it and now have the ability to help someone else make it through, that's the beauty of living a life free and forever. Scripture tells us that everything is working together for our good. Michal Chesal created Baby K'Tan because her son was born with Down Syndrome and low muscle tone. She had problems finding carriers for her child and that pushed her to tap into purpose and destiny. This lets me know that **God has the ability to make even the worst of our days better us in ways we could not have imagined.**

Well, I'm here to tell you, this is that time! You have been hidden for far too long! Now its time to pick up the pieces of your life, put them together and create the perfect picture of purpose. The days of procrastination have ended! It's time to embrace your transition. Get excited about what is about to be revealed!! Remember that all you can do means absolutely nothing until you release it. It's time to live free and forever!!

Chapter 2
Know Your Box

Imagine a life with limitless possibilities. Imagine a life where you can have everything you want. Or you could be anything you want. Vacation on exotic islands. Spend money when and how you would like to, without the aftermath of overspending. Can you imagine living a life where you wake up and decide you don't like the scenery for the day, so you call the airlines, book the flight of your choice destination and "poof".... you're in the city, state, or even country of your choice? Or maybe your desire is to help those in need. Spend time and money making sure the homeless have clothes, food and even shelter. What if you were able to help everyone that crossed your path that was in a financial bind? What if you were able to meet the needs of close friends, family members or the less fortunate because, well quite frankly, it's just in you to help and you can? What a life that would be!!! Right???

Well, the question is, what's stopping you? Who told you *that life* was not for you? What is it that is keeping this life from manifesting for you? Because you do know, there are people that live this way on an everyday basis? And I'm not only talking about the movie stars, athletes and/or your favorite music artists. There are those that you would consider to be an "Average Joe" or "Plain Jane" living the life that you dream of everyday. Studies show that there were 300,000 new millionaires created in the year of 2015 alone. So, why weren't you one of them?

The good news is, whether you know it or not, you have another level in you. There is more in you than you can imagine at this point. And I'm sure by now the millionaire on the inside of you is knocking on the glass ceiling. The greater that's on the inside of you is kicking and screaming to come out!!! I can hear it now! "Let me out!!!! Let's do it!!! Come on!!! Let's go!!!!" It's screaming from your inner parts. **Can you hear it? It's your future crying out, telling you it's okay to bet on you!!** We live in a society where it's easy to bet on everything and everyone else except yourself. None of which we have the ability to control. Hmmmm.... why would you bet on something you cannot control before you bet on the one thing you have absolute control of, yourself?

What you have on the inside of you has to be released. It can no longer be stored or hidden. It's the reason why you were born. That thing is designed to help you live your best life and make your mark in history. You were created to be great!! You were never designed to settle. God would not place anything on the inside of you that would not benefit mankind. Nor will He give you something that would waste your time and not benefit you as well. That means if He gave it to you, it will be a success. In the foreknowledge of God, He knew mankind would have specific questions at this time. So He purposed for you to be born in this day and age and impregnated you with answers that they need. Can you see how this plays out? You must know that there is a set audience that is sitting at the stage of your life waiting on the greater you to show up. And for far too long you've been a "no call, no show" because you've settled for living a life beneath your means. Even in corporate America that warrants termination! Please don't get fired on your day off!!!

Tap in! Encourage yourself. You can no longer keep responding to your greatness with a negative message. How many times have you told yourself that your idea won't work? How many times have you told yourself nobody will buy your product? And you've made this statement because of what? **The greatest asset to your future has become your biggest liability.** Just as fast as you could tell yourself you could be more, you responded with why you haven't yet become more. Or you thought about what it would take to get to that place and then convinced yourself, you didn't have what it takes. Some of you even decided that what you have at this time is enough to start but not enough to last you where you're going. Do you realize what you have done? Well, congratulations! You just officially complained in advance about something that may or may not happen. You contaminated the gift of the present with filthy thoughts of the future. Let that marinate for a second.... I'll wait.

The idea of complaining in advance sounds crazy!!! Why would you look into the future and see failure instead of success? Sure, looking ahead you should be able to see some obstacles. But they are not there to stop you. You can still move forward along the course. In fact, those obstacles are only set up to test your speed and endurance. And trust me, anything that comes fast will leave faster. But it's something about working hard and waiting for a thing that causes you to hold on to it longer. I remember the first car I had. My parents paid for most of it. Truth be told, I only worked for 2 weeks before I got it. I hated it. The day I found out that car was no good was probably the best day of my life back then. Fast forward a few years. I had a new job and worked a countless number of hours to buy the car that I wanted. For those months, I missed parties, other social gatherings and I wasn't able to come and go as I pleased. Finally, I had saved up enough money to get my own car. And even though it turned out to be a lemon, I fought long and hard to keep it. Why? Because I had overcome several obstacles to get it and I'd be John Brown before I give it away!

You must believe in yourself. Proverbs 23:7 says, "For as a man thinks in his heart, so is he." You see your perception of yourself is everything. The way you see you shows by the life you are living now. This doesn't mean that in order to be successful you need to be arrogant or prideful. This means that before you are successful, you need to see success in you. Then go pursue it! So the question is, how do YOU see YOU??? What do you believe about YOU?? When the spies were sent to see the promise land, they were instructed to bring a report back. After forty days of being in the land, they came back with evidence and a report. They brought grapes as evidence to prove the land was fruitful. They even confirmed the land was flowing with milk and honey. It indeed was the place God had promised them. But their report was, the men there were giants and they were like grasshoppers in their own eyes! In other words, it was a tall task, but they were too small to do it.

Often times we have been told by others and reminded repeatedly of our flaws and failures. You know, that time you didn't get it right. That time it didn't work. The one thing you hate about yourself seems to be the one thing that everyone has to discuss. Ever been there? And over time the weight of negativity begins to outweigh the positive truth you know about yourself. You start recycling the hurt and disappointments! But all that does is reduce the size of the giant in you mentally. That in return, will minimize the greatness that comes out of you. So when you see the promised land or the thing God has created you to do, you find yourself confessing that you cannot complete the task. And if you don't believe that you can do it, then surely you won't pursue it.

There was a class that I taught a year ago and I remember asking everyone to close their eyes and see themselves where they would want to be in life five years from now. The whole room lit up with smiles shortly after. You could feel the greater waking up on the inside of them and they loved what they were seeing. I then had them call it out. Say what they saw. The bigger the dream for one, pushed the other person's dream limitations. They called out houses, spouses and businesses of their own. It was amazing!!! They were all excited. They could see it. They said it. And then I asked them to open their eyes. One by one, the smiles begin to leave. After a short while, they were back into "reality". I then asked the question, what changed? I mean, to be honest, they were literally in the same place they were in when I told them to close their eyes. Absolutely nothing had changed. Yet excuses begin to flow like water. From the lack of finances, to not enough time, to spouses being hinderances, and even all the way to the sad truth of, "I just don't believe I can."

At the end of the day, every reason you can think of that is keeping you from pursuing your best self, has become a box. It is the very thing that is keeping you in that place you are in now. It's hiding the greatness that you have on the inside. And even as you move from your last place and take a step into your new one, remember **you were created to be great**. You were created to leave a mark in history. Greatness should never be boxed in. It has to be released, set free, to reach the highest altitude and produce its greatest product. It's the lasting image that speaks for your lifetime. It's the dash that's between your birthdate and day you leave this earth. So, what is it that is causing you to settle for living inside a box?

Application

Take a moment to list four reasons why you are not where you want to be in life. Then take two pieces of paper. Fold each piece into three sections. Open both of them up and create a bi-fold line down the middle. Then place one on top of the other to make a "X". Take the ends and fold them up. You should be looking at an open box. On each side of your box, write the 4 words that you listed previously. Congratulations, you've just been introduced to your BOX!!!

Chapter 3
"F" Is For Failure

There are several things that could possibly be holding you back right now in your life. I'm sure your list has its own validity. But right now, I want to focus on the four most common issues that people run into. Why four? Because there are four walls to a box. And now it's time to kick the walls down on your box and let them become your foundation to build on. Here are the obstacles people are dealing with the most anytime they try to pursue the "greater" in themselves: Finances, Faith, Family and Friends. Some way, shape, form or fashion, either of these components will be a hurdle you will have to jump in your life if you want to succeed.

Finances

Let's start with the biggest hurdle of them all, finances. "The lack of money is the root of all evil," says Mark Twain. It is the leading cause of stress. Studies show that 75% of Americans are stressed about money some of the time and 32% of Americans do not eat healthy because of the lack of money. Wow. Imagine that. Seems as if the world would be a better place if we all had more money. Hmmm....

So, here's the dilemma. How do I make more money if I don't have enough money to invest? You know the old saying, it takes money to make money. I'm reminded of a biblical story where there was a widow who was struggling financially. She was in the process of losing everything she owned (including her sons) to her creditors. The bible says that this woman went to ask the prophet for help in her time of need. His response to her was perplexing at first. He asked, "What do you have in your home?" Crazy, right?

As you can expect the woman was confused. Here she was, in the worst possible state she could be in at the time and he wanted to know what she had in her home! I mean, think about it, she was literally about to lose everything. So, does it really matter what she has? Besides, it's only a matter of time before what she has belongs to someone else. But then she remembers she has some oil. Not much, but she does have something to work with. He instructs her to get all the empty vessels she could find and fill them up with oil. When she's finished, sell the oil and live off of the rest of the money.

After obeying the instructions, she supernaturally went from being in debt, struggling financially, about to lose everything, to becoming a successful business woman. She made enough money to pay off all of her debt and was still able to take care of herself and sons for the rest of their lives. And believe it or not, it's really that easy (see 2 Kings 4). All you have to do is find the thing you have now, and begin to work it. Most likely it's the thing you do naturally. The thing that comes easily to you and you have been taking it for granted. Acting as if it's normal. So, the problem is not what you are doing with it. The problem could be that you're doing it for free. Or could it be you don't charge according to the value of the service. This woman knew the value of oil, and even though she was in between a rock and a hard place, she sold her item based on its value, not her condition.

Now for some, it may happen overnight and for others it may take more time. But the fact of the matter is, you have enough to start now to be successful NOW. If you're waiting on everything to perfectly line up, then you'll never move. It doesn't work that way. This is a step-by-step journey. The bible says that the steps of a good man are ordered by The Lord (Psalms 37:23). That means God orders you to step. He tells you when and how to move. Sometimes you will get instructions as you step. Your only job is to step as He releases the orders. It's God's job to make sure you have something there to catch you as your feet hit the ground. You just need to take the leap of faith. The next piece of the puzzle will arrive AFTER you take the step. So, my question is, what do you have that you can work now?

I remember a time in my life when I was preparing to start my own printing business. At the time, I was a warehouse manager at a freight forwarding company and according to my plan, I would start the business in the Spring and let the business force me to quit. Well, that was my plan. The way it actually happened was I was released for some crazy reason and received unemployment on my time off. I had not saved the money to start the business and the bills were still coming in.

I was at a crossroads in my life. But I had to make a decision. I took the money I had and invested in my dream. It was hard. I was not financially prepared. I wasn't sure where my next check was coming from. And to be honest, wasn't sure if I was going to be successful in the venture I was stepping into. But I did it. And let me tell you, the freedom of owning my own business was great! The liberty of working to fulfill my dreams was amazing. But the financial success that came with my investment was mind-blowing. It empowered my kids to believe in their dreams as well. It allowed me to spend more time with my family and do things that were in my heart but I was not able to do because I was tied to a nine to five.

So, financially things won't always make sense. It won't always look like you planned it. And to be honest, you may have to come out of the box when it doesn't make sense. You may have to knock this wall down against all odds. But when you do, you will definitely unlock another level and propel yourself towards your financial goal. If you're going to move any way, let that way be forward.... Even if it is against all odds! Kick the wall of finances down!!!

Faith

Which leads me to my next hurdle: faith. I initially wanted to talk about fear but I believe when you have enough faith, fear is not an issue. Your faith should literally cancel out your fears. Someone once said that fear is just false evidence appearing real. If that's the case, the very thing you are afraid of is not even real. Think about it. Why would you fear what doesn't exist? If you are going to be afraid of what's not real, you should add the "boogyman" to your list as well.

Now, of course we know, that faith is the substance of things hoped for and the evidence of things not seen (*Hebrews 11:1*). In layman's terms, faith is all you have until you get the very thing you are believing for. It's your belief system. Faith speaks to you on your darkest days. It reminds you of why you started in the first place. Then, it reveals to you what you are working for. Faith says, "Yes, you can!" Even when life tries to scream, "NO YOU CAN'T!" When used correctly, faith works like a guarantee. You have to remind yourself that you are guaranteed to succeed by faith. There's no way you can lose in doing the thing you were created to do. **When you learn to believe you can obtain what you are working for, nothing can stop you. And that makes you UNSTOPPABLE!!!**

Being unstoppable does not mean it will be easy. Things will arise all the time. You cannot allow trials and difficulties to make you become double-minded. The word literally means to have two minds. In one mind, you believe and in the other you don't. Can you imagine the strain that would cause on you mentally? The bible says in James 1:8 that a double minded man is unstable in all of his ways and let him expect nothing from The Lord. Could that be the reason why things have not gotten better for you? Could it be that you have reached a place that mentally you believe some days and other days you don't? It literally ties the hands of God and therefore causes Him to do nothing for you. Think about that. You are going to have to move by faith at all times and believe you have greater in you and you can live life outside of the box.

It also puts your hands and feet in shackles and chains. It keeps you from moving in any direction. At one moment, your mind is saying "Go!" And the next moment, that same mind tells you to stay. It's a confusing place to be in. Now we know that God is not the author of confusion. He came to make sure you live your best life and promises to direct you if you lean not to your own understanding. That takes an effort to trust God in everything. That's the only way you can be free and live forever!

So, do you believe you have "greater" in you? If you do, how strong is your faith? **Life will always present challenges. And challenges will always present themselves as you're moving in the right direction.** The disciples found themselves in that same predicament in Matthew chapter 14. At the words of Jesus, they decided to take a leap of faith. They found themselves moving in what they believed to be the right direction. About halfway there, a storm broke out and the bible says that the wind began to blow contrary. Can you imagine how their faith was being tested? In the constant pursuit of moving forward there was an invisible force blowing them the opposite direction.

At that moment, they had to make a conscious decision to keep going forward or turn around. I'm sure the initial consensus was to head the other way. I mean, by now, it's hard for them to see where they're going. And every effort for them to keep going is becoming harder and harder. The issue had now become more than physical, it was now mental as well. Can you imagine the strain? The fatigue? The frustration? Yet, they believed. They continued to move forward because they believed that what they were pursuing would be reached.

Their faith was so strong that they continued to try even though they didn't see any results. Guess what? God met them right where they were. He showed up in the nick of time. In the middle of their biggest storm, he showed up and made everything alright. He responded to their faith. You see in order to be greater, you have to believe on a greater level. At the end of the day, your faith will be all you have until what you are waiting on manifests. **Don't lose your faith. Your leap of faith may lead you to the worst storm of your life, but keep believing and know that God will meet you right where you are.**

Now, Jesus was not in the boat as they left, but He met them in the middle of the sea. Can you imagine what would have happened if they turned around? Or what would have happened if they decided to stop where they were? You see, although God is all knowing He has a plan to meet you where you need Him most. The purpose of releasing a word to the disciples is to test their faith. Remember, without faith it is impossible to please God. (Hebrews 11:6) So, as it got harder, He started on His journey to meet them in a specific place. And as their faith was being tested, they were in route to the greatest miracle of their life. It took belief to keep them moving. And the fact that they did positioned them for a breakthrough of all time!!!

My mother, to me, has the craziest faith I have ever seen! I have seen her consistently believe God in the face of adversity and never relinquish her stance. She now has, what she calls, a "faith trophy case" in which she keeps all of her testimonies of the impossible that God has done for her. I am always honored and amazed as I sit at her feet from time to time and listen to the countless number of victories she has won on faith alone!!

But there is one particular story that stands out to me. There was a time in her life when she desired for a new vehicle. Now at this particular time, her credit score was low and to complicate things, she was also unemployed. Yet, she still wanted a new vehicle. Crazy, right? Well, the story goes on and she attends her usual Sunday morning church service. She said that day church was pretty normal until her Pastor stood up and said that the favor of God was at the dealership. And by faith she received it.

The very next day she made a trip to the car lot. She said the salesman approached her as they normally would. She strolled the lot until she found the vehicle she wanted. She proceeded to tell the young man her situation and then pointed out the car that she would like to have. Of course, the salesman is confused. He's trying to figure out two things:

1. Why would you come to the car lot with no money down and bad credit?

2. How are you going to finance a car that you are not working to pay for?

Well, needless to say, the only response she had was, by faith God will make a way. Hours passed and they actually entertained the idea of giving her a car. They reached out to see if banks would even finance her while in her current position. Conversations were held and before the day was over, I received a phone call. It was my mom. She wanted me to come outside of my house to see her new car!!! My mom got the car! The only stipulations the car lot had was, she had thirty days to bring the down payment back. Well, within the week, she received a phone call for a job opportunity and got hired. Her first check was enough to pay tithes, bills and the down payment!!!

You see, **in order to receive the unbelievable, you are going to have to believe the unbelievable can happen!** Against all odds, your faith has to be the thing that motivates you to pursue your desires. God is obligated to respond to faith, nothing else. The bible says that all things are possible to him that believes! So, the question is, do you have the faith to come out of the box? Because if you take a step, God will honor your faith and reward you for it. He will never let you down, just try Him!!!

Family

You have to know who you are and where you came from. I was always taught that family is everything and blood is thicker than water. I'm not disagreeing with that or even debating it, but I will say that at some point you may have to break the status quo. Think about it, how many people in your family are successful now? How many millionaires are you connected to? If your answer is zero, then you definitely have some work to do. I'm a firm believer that exposure brings closure to dreams. In other words, you need to be exposed to what it is that you are trying to obtain. Seeing it being done on a successful level always sets a new fire ablaze. But what if the example is not within your family? Then your family tree can be another wall that needs to be knocked down.

Even Jesus Himself had to deal with this issue. The 13th chapter of Matthew tells a story of Jesus entering His hometown. It talks about Him teaching and performing miracles. The people were amazed but they still had an issue. You see, even though Jesus was doing great things, they could only think about who He was, based on what they knew about His family. They asked questions amongst themselves like, "Isn't this Mary's son. Isn't that Joseph, the carpenter's son." They began to call out the name of His brothers and make mention of His sisters. You see, they had put Jesus in a box based off of who His family was. The bible ends the chapter by saying He did not many works there because of their unbelief. What a sad day in history. To have the greatest man that ever walked the earth placed in a box, simply because His family didn't fit the definition of being great.

You would think, the fact that His teaching was astounding and the fact that He performed miracles there would be enough evidence to believe in Him. But it wasn't the case. You see you could have a great plan, talk until you're blue in the face, and even prove that your plan works, but it still won't make people believe in you. Especially if they know who you are or where you come from. People need to have a point of reference. And if they can't see it in you, then they will begin to look for it in your family. You start stepping outside of the box and start talking about this million dollars you are about to make and it will be a foreign language to some people. They're trying to figure out how you can do what has never been done in your family's history. What makes you so special? **It's crazy how your family tree can unknowingly place a cap on your potential.**

I listened to Jada Pinkett Smith tell a portion of her testimony recently. All of it was good, but there was one thing that stood out to me. The host asked her why her and her husband, Will Smith, were so committed to helping young aspiring actors. What she said was mind blowing. She began to talk about the struggles they had when they first came into acting. And the truth of the matter was, acting was never their issue. But she mentioned the term "first generation wealth". They had never seen so much money before. Nobody in their family had ever made that kind of money before! It was all new to them. They were the first! So, they needed help with properly managing large amounts of cash. What a beautiful problem to have, right? **Can you see yourself, breaking past the glass ceiling of your family tree limitations to create first generational wealth?** The moral of the story is to not let what you see in your family keep you from chasing your dreams! You may have to be the first!!! Somebody has to do it, might as well be you!!!

Let's turn the page for a second and look at Matthew chapter 12. Here you find Jesus walking in His assignment, doing the thing He was called to do. But in verse 46 something interesting happens. In the middle of Him teaching, He gets word that His "family" is outside and they want to speak with Him. It is at this moment Jesus has to make a decision to either do what He was commissioned to do or either stop and go see what His family wanted. Torn between the assignment and the commitment, Jesus makes one of the toughest decisions of His life at the time. Now mind you, His mother and everyone are all out there. And we all know how "mom" has a special place in her son's heart. Right?

But Jesus does not respond. Instead, He makes a bold statement and says he or she that is doing my fathers will, they are my family. He then continues doing what He was doing. What a declaration? Jesus was so committed to living a life free and forever that He was willing to become a part of a new family. At first glance, it seems as if He is turning His back on family. You know that's a pretty harsh thing to do; ignore your family when they are calling you. But that's not what He was doing at all. Look again. He was simply acknowledging those who were walking closest with Him as family. And though He hadn't known them as long, He knew they were going to play a part in His destiny and they needed to be treated accordingly. And those who knew Him, although they loved Him, were being a distraction at the time. Now I believe they weren't doing it on purpose. Most family members don't. But if they don't understand what you are doing, they can unknowingly become another wall on your box!!!

You are going to have to make a conscious decision to keep family in their rightful place. As you begin to step out the box, there will be times that family will have something to say about it. They have a way of trying to make their presence and their opinions known. Know that your coming out of the box is a personal thing. It's a decision that YOU are making for YOU. So You will have to stay committed to what YOU are doing for YOU. Sometimes family will not understand the magnitude of what you are trying to accomplish. Jesus was preparing His disciples to take the gospel worldwide. What you are coming out of the box for is going to leave a mark in this world as well. It will make sure that you live forever! Please don't let them interrupt your pursuit of destiny. Stay focused. Treat those who are designed to work with you as family. Keep the understanding that they are there on purpose. And their commitment deserves your loyalty.

They say that real family ties are the hardest to break. Growing up as a young teen, my family and I spent a lot of time together as a family. My aunt was like my second mom. My cousins were like the little brothers and sisters I did not have. We were so close that my younger cousins would call my mom "mom" and address their mom as "auntie"! We thought it was funny, but she hated it! My friends to this day still respect and treat my parents as their own because we were that close. We spent that much time together and if you knew me, you knew them.

Fast forward in time, and I eventually gave my life to Christ. Although many were in shock, surprisingly, it was a move that forced my siblings and other family members to make life changing decisions as well, because we were that close. We began hosting bible study at my house and family prayer meetings. Over time, I believe that God led us all to the same church. And we then, studied, prayed and worshipped together. Oh what a time!!

Everything was great... and then my wife and I decided to change churches. The rest of the family would eventually change churches as well. And by God's divine plan, they would all end up at the same church again, with the exception of me and my family. You see I had found a new church that was giving me "life"! The teaching was like no other! I was introduced to so many things of God and blessed to serve and sit under some Kingdom Giants. Our church schedules were different. We had different bible study nights and honestly, we were in church a lot more than they were. It took away from the time we would spend together. In that place, I had to decide what was more important to me. Was it going to be the comfortable place of family time or pursue destiny. It caused me to have to see the people that played a major part in my future as family. And for a while my normal was broken. What was knitted together so tightly was seemingly coming undone at the seams. But kicking down that wall of my box is what set the foundation of where I am now, writing this book about living free and forever.

Think it not strange if you have to replace the old with new. It's not popular and to be honest, it may be the hardest thing you'll have to do. But if you stay focused on your path, purpose and destiny, it will all make sense in the end. **Don't**

allow the familiar to keep you from experiencing the foreign. Just keep in mind, familiar is where you are now and foreign is a place where you have never been. If you were ok with where you are, then you wouldn't be reading this book. True story!

Friends

Friends. How many of us have them? Friends. Ones we can depend on? There's a powerful statement that birds of a feather, flock together. Meaning that like-minded people somehow find themselves hanging together. So, coming out of the box is going to challenge all of your friendships. As long as you are comfortable with being comfortable, those around you will remain comfortable as well. But the minute you decide you want more, those closest around you will be affected the most. It will be amazing to see how your desire for more opens your eyes to people's complacency for less.

So, when's the last time you did a circle check? I mean seriously evaluated those who are around you. Paul writes in his letter to Corinth that bad company corrupts good character (1 Corinthians 15:33). He was teaching them a principle that is still relevant today. Be careful of who you hang around because eventually you all will have the same mindset. Walk with the wise and become wise, for a companion of fools suffers harm (Proverbs 13:20). Everyone around doesn't have to be scholars, but they should all be pursuing an out of the box experience that is going to have them living their life free and forever.

This couldn't be more true for a young man in the bible. 1 Kings 13 tells a story of a young prophet who was living life outside of the box. He was given instructions from God and seeing immediate fruits from it. It's always funny to me how the word of success travels and attracts the worst of people. This story was no different. His fame had spread and now an old prophet was on his way to find him. Even though the young prophet knew what his purpose was, he still allowed the older man to talk him into doing something he knew he wasn't supposed to do. The bad company corrupted the good character of the younger man and eventually caused him to lose his life.

You are going to have to see your company from the vantage point of whether or not this person benefits or hinders your life. Make your decision as if your life depends on it. Because, let's face it, it does! **People have a way of becoming the greatest distraction to those who want to be great.** They somehow have this ability to feed on the circumstances of life and because of that, they can push you into making a fatal choice. The young prophet was given the instruction to not eat in the places he was sent. But after doing the work of The Lord, I'm sure he had worked up an appetite. The old prophet convinced the man to come to his house and eat. People are looking for an opening into your life. And too often, your current void becomes an entrance to your life. So, you are going to have to make sure you have the right people around you at all times. Now there's no need to remove everybody; no man is an island, but you are definitely going to have to remove the bad company if you want your life to stay incorruptible.

Often times we fail to realize the power of influence people have over us. Those that are closest to you, will have a front row seat to your life. And as a forewarning, living outside of the box will have you doing some crazy things. If people aren't in tune with the vision God has given you or what you are trying to pursue, they will try to talk you out of what you are doing. Remember, nobody that loves anybody wants to see that person go through a hard phase for any period of time. Don't believe me. Ask Job. Job was going through the most difficult time of his life. Job had tapped into his greater and was living his best life. Then tragedy struck. He lost everything. And in that moment, he could have made a decision to do something different. Friends began to come by and beg and plead that he change his mind about his decision. I believe they were good people. They just hated to see Job struggle. But he didn't and eventually was rewarded with double. If you stick to your goals, you too can receive a life that is better than you have ever dreamed of.

As you know, not all friends are bad. Some people really do have your best interest at heart. David at a young age was anointed to be king. Saul, who was king at the time, unknowingly allowed David to remain close because David played music that would give Saul peace in his times of distress. He also was a great leader of the army and won many battles for Saul. Now, Jonathan was the oldest son of Saul. I believe it was during the time of serving Saul, David and Jonathan became close. As a matter of fact, they became the best of friends.

Well, David's fame grew. The people began to praise David more than they praised Saul. And this made Saul highly upset. He was upset to the point that he wanted to kill David. Imagine the conflict this would bring in between David and his best friend Jonathan. Jonathan did everything in his power to keep his dad from trying to kill David. But, there came a time when he had to make a decision on behalf of David's future. He realized that where David was at the time was becoming a "box" that would eventually kill him. So, he devised a plan that would release David to his greater and let him live free and forever.

It was hard for Jonathan to believe that his dad wanted to kill David. So, he asked David to hide in a field until he confirmed whether or not the story was true. He was going to shoot three arrows into the field and have a servant go get them. Depending on his description of where the arrows landed would let David know if it was safe for him to remain in the country or if he needed to leave. So, at the appointed time, he did exactly what he said. Facing the harsh reality of his father's anger towards David, he advised him to leave the country. You see, a real friend will never place limits on you. They will always see where you are going. And even though getting there requires you to move beyond the limits of their friendship, they will never keep you in the box. It doesn't always require a complete letting go of the good friends you have but sometimes you have to put some distance in between the two of you in order to live your best life.

I remember running the streets as a child and meeting some very influential people in my life. These guys had the money, power and respect. The more I connected with them, the more they would tell me to leave my circle and get new friends. It made no sense. As much as I wanted what they had, the idea of turning my back on my friends was unbearable. I mean, how could I live with myself? These guys were there for me no matter what! They helped me build what I had established. It just didn't feel like the right thing to do, you know? So, I found myself constantly evaluating my circle. I watched more carefully the difference between the two circles. How we moved as a group versus how they moved. The respect they had in the streets against the respect we got. I mean the money, women and lifestyle was totally different, yet we were involved in the same thing. What did they have that my friends didn't? It wasn't until 5 years later that I would fully understand that statement.

You see as good as my friends were to me, we were all on the same level. And I had maxed out with them. They were great, and still are, but nothing was happening in my immediate circle that pushed me to do more. We all had a car, pretty nice. Had a little clientele so we made some money but it wasn't that extravagant amount, you know, nothing to brag about! And the truth of the matter is, they were the glass ceiling over my head that was keeping me from going to that next level (Thank God). The moral of the comment was, if you hang around better, you'll do better. Someone had seen the potential I had and my circle didn't match it. Not because they were bad people or incapable of reaching that next place but because they weren't already there.

I did eventually change my circle. They all had jobs and worked for a living. So, I did too. They all drove nice cars and dressed the part... guess what.. I did too. They invested in rims, tvs and sound systems for their car and I did too. Now, I didn't start off on that level but the more I hung around them, the more I realized I needed to step my game up to their level if we were going to hang out on a regular basis. They pushed me out of my comfort zone and it was a great transition for me to enter into God's Kingdom.

Failure is never an option.

If you think about it, it should be pretty hard to fail. When you find yourself doing what you were created to do and you have tapped into your purpose, it should be hard not to complete your God-given assignment. To not complete the task, says that you are not working properly. Once you flip the light switch, the light bulb does not shine automatically. There is a flow of power that must be released. But when it is working properly, it has the ability to light up the whole room. It's fulfilling its purpose. Now any time it does not, the thought that comes to mind is, maybe the bulb is broken. That's how life views you when you are not fulfilling purpose. Maybe you are broken. Maybe somewhere along the way, something has become distorted and you are not sure what you should be doing right now. Any time you find yourself in that place, you leave a vacancy in the earth. What you have to offer is an ingredient that is designed to make a difference. But you have somehow become out of order, not working properly. And the ingredient you were supposed to add to the world's gumbo has been left out. It just might be the reason why things are going the way they are. Maybe.

If failure is not an option, then quitting can't be one either. I have come to realize, most people don't fail, they quit. If you are going to reach your goals, you must have a "no quit" in you. No matter what happens, don't give up. There must be a fight in you like no other. You are literally fighting for your life. Your best life at that! But maybe your calculated cost of greatness is too much. The price of your next level is not worth paying and you would rather live in mediocrity. Your goals must be attainable. Success doesn't happen overnight. Businesses don't grow over night either. To expect to be a millionaire at the end of your first year is outrageous. Paul uses the analogy of a man swinging aimlessly at a target that cannot be hit. It brings unnecessary fatigue, frustration and disappointment. Neither are conducive attributes to success. Most financial advisers would say that it takes a minimum of two years of running your own business before you can start to really see the fruits of your labor. If that be true, you would have to go into it with the expectation of working for free for two years.

Now there is a difference between failing and making a mistake. I believe it's easy to make a mistake, but your mistakes should never outweigh your drive to complete the task at hand. **A mistake only proves two things, one that you're human, and two, that the way you just tried didn't work. In either case, your mistake shouldn't define you, it should refine you.** Let it make you better rather than prove you don't have what it takes to complete the assignment. In 1953, the Rocket Chemical Company and its staff set out to make their mark in history. They were determined to live free and forever. After failing 39 times, they finally came up with the right formula to make what we know now as WD40, which stands for Water Displacement Perfected on the 40th try. Mistakes are bound to happen but it doesn't have to be your final destination as long as you continue to move forward!!! You can reach your goals!!!

    Make the choice today. Choose YOU and your best life. Lay aside your financial insecurities and start with what you have now. Have faith that you can make it and against all odds you will rise to the top. Don't let your DNA give you an identity that keeps you in a box. You may be the first millionaire in the family. Be okay with being that. Live as if you are setting a new standard for your bloodline. Get you a team that's willing to walk this out with you and treat them as family.

    Understand the power of influence your friends have on you. If they're not pushing you out of the box, they're keeping you in it. Failure is not an option. If you can master these four areas, I believe you will be well on your way to living free and forever.

Application

1. Based on the previous chapter, where do the following areas rank in your life as it relates to keeping you in the box (1 being the highest, 4 being the lowest)?
    a. Family
    b. Friends
    c. Finances
    d. Faith
2. Write at least 4 limitations each area presents.

Chapter 4
You Only Get An "E" For Effort... That's All

You're knocking down walls. Making a conscious decision to come out of the box. You're building a solid foundation by overcoming the limitations of finances, faith, family and friends. Yet, you are still in the same place. So, what now? At least now, you can see opportunity to move forward. Joe Namath said something so powerful. He said, "If you're not going to go all the way, why go at all?"

It's been debated which step is the hardest. Is it the first step across the starting line, or the last step over the finish line? You see most believe if they could just start, they'll gain momentum. And if they can gain momentum, they'll have enough strength to finish at the end. So, the first step is critical. It determines how the rest of the race will be run. If you start incorrectly, you will find yourself running just to catch up. You'll find yourself wasting energy and time. Then life outside of the box becomes more frustrating and depressing than life inside the box. But when you start correctly, the race becomes easier. Each stride flows into the next. You gather a rhythm that makes the next task easier to conquer. But be mindful, this is a marathon, not a sprint! You're going to have to endure!!

So, let me give you some basic principles for making your first step out of the box.

1. **Eliminate** any and everything that reminds you of your box. When Elijah put the mantle on Elisha, Elisha knew that there was something greater out there for him. Before he pursued that place, the bible says he went back, kissed his family and burned all of his equipment. He was stating by action, that this is all I'm going after and by no way am I returning to this place again. Getting rid of every reminder, helps you stay focused and ensures that you won't go back to where you came from (1 Kings 19:19-21).

2. **Evaluate** what you have and who's around you. The widow was given specific instructions from the prophet once she realized what she had in the house. She was told to go to her neighbors and borrow vessels to fill. Then, take the vessels, and go home. Only her and her sons were allowed in the house and she was told to shut the door. Now I would love to imagine the evaluating process she had to go through. She had to think about what she had and who she could borrow from. From there, make a clear distinction of who she would take in the house with her. Begin to take inventory of what you have, who

you know and who you are going to allow close to you as you prepare to live out of the box (2 Kings 4:1-7).

3. **Educate** yourself. The bible says that we perish for a lack of knowledge (Hosea 4:6). To not know, is to not grow. Whatever God has placed in your heart, begin to research the ins and outs of the vision. Learn every aspect of the field. Study to see what worked and why. Also, learn about the failures of the business as well. Paul tells Timothy to study to show himself approved (2 Timothy 2:15). You are going to have to be able to cover every area of the business, knowledge wise, if you want to be approved in your field or profession. It's the work before the work!!!

4. **Enter** a plan. One of the biggest mistakes people make is going into a thing without a plan. Habakkuk was told to write the vision and make it plain.... For surely it will come to pass (Habakkuk 2:2). Take the time to make a step by step plan for your journey. Cover every detail and plan as if you are going to have to obtain everything you need. Make it very plain. Write it as if you are explaining it to someone who knows absolutely nothing about what you're doing. But make sure you are detailed enough for them to be able to complete your vision as if you were doing it.

It's going to take a new effort to come out of the box. You're going to have to tap into a strength that is far greater than yours. Effort is described to be a vigorous or determined attempt at a thing. It can either be mental or physical. The bible says in 1 John, "Greater is He that is in me, than he that's in the world." (1 John 4:4) You have to believe there is someone greater on the inside of you. But know that He's not just there because He doesn't have anywhere else to be. He's there to help you. He'll help you every step of the way. When you feel as if your strength is not enough, tap into the "greater" that's in you!!!

It is so easy to rely on your own strength. After all, your whole life has taught you to become stronger to conquer. But every emotional letdown, only made you stronger. The day your heart was broken, it hurt, but somehow you became stronger because of it. If you were involved in sports, you trained harder to become stronger. And if you're like me, you measured your progress by the pain you felt the next morning. But I want to suggest a new way to become stronger, become weak. Wait... I'll give you a minute to re-read that sentence again. Yes, I said become weak, to become stronger. Paul acknowledges his shortcomings to God on a repeated basis. Only to find out, that God would not remove the thorn in his flesh that was making him weak. Instead, he learned that God's power was made perfect in his weaknesses (2 Corinthians 12:9). It became flawless. Not that there is an issue with God's power. But it was in that place, he learned how to allow God's power to do all the work. And it worked perfectly.

Don't be afraid to let your weaknesses be known to God. Trust His power in them, it's flawless!

He's working in you. He's also working for you. And the beauty of it all is that He gives you the strength to carry it out in the natural. The bible says He [God] has given you the power to get wealth (Deuteronomy 8:18). It was never His intention for you to struggle financially. He created you for a specific purpose and ordained you to carry it out in the earth realm. Think of it this way, every wealthy person you can think of is known for a specific reason. If I say Michael Jordan, you'll say basketball. If I say Bill Gates, you'll say Microsoft. Or if I say Facebook, you'll say Mark Zuckerberg. You see each of these individuals have tapped into the power to create wealth. They invested in themselves some way, shape, form, or fashion and made a conscious decision to leave their mark in history. Some may be more important to others depending on the need of the individual. But nevertheless, all three individuals have made an impact on life as we know it. And it's simply because they learned how to become powerful!! They had a vision, dream and a plan and then they used their God given power to create it, and it made them very wealthy!!!

So where is your wealth? Why haven't you seen it yet??? I'm sure you're wondering just what you need to do to get the life you were born to live. I'll tell you. It's the dream you leave on the shelf every day to remain comfortable. There is a quote that says, "If you don't build your dream, someone will hire you to help build theirs." That's right, your wealth is attached to the thing you have been putting off for years. That's what that power was designed to do. You just have to believe that you have the power. There's nothing you cannot do. All things are possible to him who believes (Mark 9:23). If you believe you can, YOU CAN! Believe you can create your own wealth. Believe that this decision, vision and dream is going to set you up financially for generations to come. Then tap into your greater and work from that place. **Even in your weaknesses, rely on His power, and get perfect results.** You CAN do ALL things!

But at the end of the day, you only get an "e" for effort. Trying gets you started but it doesn't get the job done. And I'm sure you can agree that a beginning without an end is pointless. **You have a reason to start but the reason to end is so much greater.** You have to ask yourself, how many times have you made a choice to start your own business, only to get comfortable with working for someone else again? How many times have you grabbed your dream off of the shelf, only to put it down again? If you want to come out of the box and succeed, give your best effort, and lean on the power of the almighty God.

I personally have made the mistake of trying and not succeeding far too many times. It has been a desire of mine to go to college and of course I've tried it. Sad to say, but I have tried it more than once. I would always start off excited! I would be there every day. Sit in the front row! Books, backpack, paper and pen in hand. In full attention and ready to learn. The first week would go by and my teachers would always speak highly of me. They would tell me how much potential I had and if I just stuck with it, I would be very successful. Well, this of course, added fuel to the fire!! Now I really wanted to be there and soak up all the wisdom they had!!!

But somewhere in between starting and finishing, life would happen. I would find myself going from being there every day to missing one or two days a week. My grades begin to show. I went from being an "A" student to a "B" student and over time I would drop down to even further than that. It wasn't that I lost the potential, it was just that my focus was off. And what started off being a plan to succeed became just an idea. A great thought that never actually happened.

Well, graduation day for my class came around. People were making plans to get cap and gowns and taking pictures and planning these extravagant parties. You could hear the congratulatory conversations going on. The excitement of finishing what you started was all in the atmosphere. Teachers high fiving students and telling them they always knew they could do it. Some teachers even apologized for not believing the student could do it. It was crazy. At least, that what I heard. You see while all this was going on, I was at home. Trying to put a rhyme and reason to why I didn't make it. But it's cool that I tried though.... Right?

Application

1. Make a list of all your areas of weakness. Some areas need to be sharpened and some areas are going to totally require God's power. Check what you can change and put a star next to those you will need God's power to change.

2. Research your new venture. Learn how to be successful in it. Never allow yourself to be in a place where you will have to reinvent the wheel.

3. Write your vision and make it plain. Step by step, put a plan together for success. I advise you to skip lines in between each step. Give God room to make changes at any time.

Chapter 5
You Can Get An "A" If You Go All the Way

Now that you have a plan in place, it's time to move forward. To get the life you are seeking after you are going to have to be persistent in your pursuit. Obstacles are going to come but your mind has to be made up that what's before you is better than what's behind you. Paul describes this mentality best! Although he had become famous for his miracles and teaching, he still thought that he had not apprehended or fully reached his potential yet. So, he learned how to forget what was behind him and continue to reach for what was in front of him. It caused him to press forward towards the mark or prize of a higher calling. Jesus came that we may have life and life more abundantly. (John 10:10) It was always God's will that you live your best life. But you must become like Paul and activate a hunger for it. He developed a mindset that said I refuse to settle for where I am now. He declared that whatever happened yesterday will not hinder his today nor will it have any effect on his tomorrow. He also understood that there would need to be a constant reaching for what he was searching for. And with that mindset, you must develop a "press" for your prize. The press is normally hard because it goes against the grain but is definitely worth the work. Make your mind up to press forward in every situation. **Never settle for where you are. There's always another level to obtain.**

Before you can press, you must first forget. The word in the original language means to overlook. There are things that have happened to you that you will never forget but you can look over them. This requires you to look from a different angle. Go higher mentally. Think on a level greater than you have thought before. Gain another view that will cause you to keep moving forward. Because if you do not, it will become a weight that makes you wait. Have you ever tried to drive or even walk forward while looking backwards? It's impossible to get to your place of destination while doing so. Somehow you will find yourself veering off to the right or left until you finally crash. Paul intentionally overlooked everything that had happened to him up until that point, just to become mentally focused on pressing towards a greater goal. You can't deny your past. Neither can you ignore the present. But you can overlook every obstacle and develop a press for success!

What does it mean to press? I like to think of it as **(P.R.E.S.S.) Pressure Released in Effort to See Success.** Living life outside of the box adds more pressure than normal.

It forces you to become uncomfortable with what is, in order to achieve what's to become. But if you don't handle the pressure correctly, the thing that's designed to bless you will feel more like a curse. It will cause you to lose sleep. Force you to change your eating habits. It comes to shake everything you believe in, with the efforts of getting results. It will challenge you in every area. So, you are going to have to handle it correctly. Be intentional. Spend your late nights preparing for the morning ahead. Eat healthier. Add a regular workout routine. Your foundation will be shaken but you have the power to build the empire you were designed to live in. Press for it! You got this!!!

There was a woman with an issue of blood in the bible. And after spending all she had and doing all she knew to do; the issue was still not fixed. She went to see the best physicians that money could offer. But it only left her broke, and on top of everything else, the issue grew worse. She was exiled from the community. Anytime she entered the public, she would have to announce what her issue was so people knew to stay away from her. But one day, she made a decision to do something different. She heard that what she needed to live free and forever was close by. And the bible says that she said to herself, "If I could just touch the hem of His [Jesus] garment, then surely I'll be made whole." (Matthew 9:20-22) She made a declaration that led to a decision. When was the last time you did that?

There were two problems in front of her at this point. The first was the crowd around Him. The fame of Jesus was spreading rapidly. Every city, town or country He entered, He would be met by the locals who were in need or just came to see a miracle. Being exiled from everyday living meant she would have to take the risk of going into public which broke all rules. What would they say? How would they respond? How would they treat her? Imagine the pressure she felt!! What was she to do? Continue living a life that was well beneath her means or *press* her way through the crowd to have her life changed forever? Decisions, decisions. Not only did she have to deal with her current condition internally but externally it brought public embarrassment to her. Everyone was well aware of what she was going through at this time. And the same people that belittled her and made her feel like life was not worth living, are the same people standing in between her and her miracle.

The second roadblock was the fact that Jesus was actually on His way somewhere else. There was a man whose daughter was dying and he needed Jesus to come to his house to heal her as well. So, Jesus, at the time, was on the move. Which meant the more she thought about it, the further away He got. The clock was ticking continuously and her space of grace was in the process of passing her by. At this point, she was going to have to make up in her mind to forget the past failures of yesterday. Forget the rules. All the money she had spent, every wrong turn and bad decision she had made up until that point needed to be overlooked. It was time to *press*!! She needed to only focus on her target. And with a made-up mind, the ability to achieve what was in front of her became more evident.

I could envision the struggle she felt. She had to move in from behind the crowd. Some people probably had to be moved out of the way. Some probably refused, so she had to take an alternate route. She could have possibly had to deal with the snickering of other individuals who recognized who she was. But she had a target. A mark that was set before her and nothing was going to stop her from getting what she needed. She was focused in her mind and in her heart, which caused her body to move. The pressure she was feeling was now being released to see success. Her plan was in motion and she would not be denied. When she finally got to Jesus, not only was she healed, but her social status was restored.

You too have been defined by your condition for far too long. Whether it be your financial status, race or sex, someone has made the assumption that you are the square that doesn't fit into the circle of life. People have already counted you out. They've written you off and went on with life as if you no longer have a voice or even exist. It's caused you to be on the outside looking in. But the rejection was your protection. It kept the treasure on the inside of you from being tainted. It is now your fueling fire for the next phase of your life. Let it burn. Let it burn brightly! Eyes have not seen your best yet! Your social status is about to be changed! **The same people that turned their backs on you are going to be in position to watch you be rewarded for your press.** And even after all of this, they too, will have to admit you have something to bring to the table and they're glad you are living life free and forever.

Just work your plan! They say that if you fail to plan, then you plan to fail. But be sensitive enough to make adjustments while never straying away from what you originally planned to do. Sounds confusing? Let me explain. Your vision is the most important thing you have. It's what you have seen, declared and are believing for that drives you every morning. But sometimes we think that it has to happen the way we wrote it down. What happens when step four presents itself before your scheduled time? Do you pass on it because it didn't happen according to your plan exactly? No. Because it is a step on your path, you pray and make sure that the timing is right. God gives a word to the prophet Habakkuk to write the vision and make it plain (Habakkuk 2:2). He instructs him that though it may tarry, surely it will come to pass. You see, you can only get what you believe for, if you are committed to working for it. Again, faith is the substance of things hoped for and the evidence of things not seen (Hebrews 11:1). Before you get it, all you have is your faith or belief that you shall obtain what you came out of the box for. But you are going to have to walk it out step by step and believe that where you are going is worth the journey.

I'm reminded of the story of the prophet and the young man who needed a healing. He became very ill and there was no cure for his disease. Because he was a man of authority, he really didn't want to leave his life and spend the rest of his days in exile. So, he got word that there was a prophet who could make his issue disappear. He goes to see the prophet and receives instructions. Unfortunately, it was not pleasing to his ears. He was told to go dip himself in the Jordan river 7 times and his condition would change. But the Jordan was dirty. Why there? At this time, he had to make a choice whether he was going to work the vision that was given to him or decide to do something different. I'm sure he thought, "What do I have to lose? If it works, I'm cured. If it doesn't, I'm still in the same condition I was in when I arrived." Well, he followed the instructions step by step. He went to the right place and dipped the right amount of times. And he got the results he was looking for (1 Kings 5:1-14).

You are going to have to trust that what God has given you is going to work. It may require you getting a little dirty but it will be worth it. **Don't allow your own logic to talk you out of obeying the instructions you have been given.**

His ways are not your ways and His thoughts are not your thoughts. As high as the heavens are from the earth, so is His thoughts above yours (Isaiah 55:8-9). If you would be honest with yourself, you can admit that it was your own logic that got you trapped inside a box. But if you can trust the vision that God gave you, you will see the results He promised. Do it step by step. Omit nothing. And gain the cure for the issues of life you have been struggling with.

Hmmm... but what happens when you struggle with trying to overcome your struggle? I can't lie, this is going to possibly be the hardest thing you will ever have to do. But the good news is, it can be done. The bible says "I can do all things through Christ which strengthens me." (Philippians 4:13) That's right, ALL!!! There isn't any limitation placed on your abilities. Whatever it is you set your mind to do, you can do it. There's only one stipulation, you're going to have to rely on Christ's strength. What a joy to know that you can tap into an all-powerful source and use it!!!

There once was a man at the gate called Beautiful with an ugly situation. You see he was lame and did not have the ability to walk. And every day someone would carry him to a place where he could professionally beg for money. Ironically, this place was right in front of the temple. It has always amazed me that the people were willing to bring him to a particular destination that would keep him codependent on others but never take him where they knew he would get his freedom. As beautiful as life is, you may still find yourself in a dilemma. It is possible that life can take all the movement out of you, causing you to feel that you are in a lame or stagnant place. Some people are born without the power to move as this man was, but there are some that encounter hardships that will literally stop all movement or momentum. Well, one day the Apostles were walking by and he asked them for a donation. Peter responded and said that he didn't have any money but what he had, he was willing to share. Peter's response didn't mean he was broke, but he recognized the man needed more than money. He was saying that all the money I have won't fix your issue but I have something that will. And right then at that moment, the man received his healing.

What did Peter give him? First, he gave him the ability to believe again. I'm sure Peter was the first to speak to his faith, although everyone that passed was going to the "house of faith" and never spoke to empower him. Nobody, until that time, had even mentioned the possibility of him being able to walk. The next thing he did was put the responsibility back on him. The man had spent his whole life waiting on someone to do something for him and now Peter was asking him to do something for himself. He wanted him to make a decision to believe on another level. Finally, he reached out his hand to grab the lame man's hand and allowed him to receive a power that he had not known. As their hands touched, Peter supernaturally transferred the healing that the man needed. The bible says that Peter helped him up and at that same moment he received strength to his feet and ankle bones. The man had officially tapped into the power that God releases and it gave him strength to get on his feet. What a wonderful sight to see! The miraculous power of God manifested right in front of your eyes! That definitely would be a beautiful sight!!!

You see God is not concerned with giving handouts. He's more focused on giving you a hand up. The old saying is you can give a man a fish and feed him for a day or you can teach him how to fish and feed him for a lifetime! God is blessing you to help you live life more abundantly. So, he intentionally gives you a power that works on the inside of you that You can't give yourself. You can't see it but you will feel it. It will overtake you supernaturally. This power is designed to help you get up and walk out your purpose in life, walk out your destiny, walk out your dreams and live your life free and forever!!!

So, tap in!! Allow God to put His super with your natural!!! It's a guaranteed recipe for success.

Jesus declares that if you abide in Him and He abides in you, then you will be able to bear much fruit. He then says that without Him you can do nothing (John 15:5). It's one thing to come out of the box but it's another to produce. Don't be afraid. God has not given you the spirit of fear, but he has given you power, love and a sound mind (2 Timothy 1:7). He designed you to be fearless and to operate in power. Just press for your prize!! Trust the instructions you received, no matter how crazy they may be. Follow them to the letter. Even if you have to take a risk at getting dirty. And most importantly, tap into a source that's greater than you! Believe you can. Know you can. And make the connection of your life!!! After all, you only get an "A", if you go ALL the way!!!!

My son is far brighter than he knows! And trust me when I tell you, he is very confident in his intellectual ability. But for some strange reason, he gets comfortable and finds himself not consistently putting his best foot forward at all times. He'll harp on the fact that he passes all of his classes! He's always on the honor roll making A's and B's but never has been able to make the all A honor roll. Now as parents, we are grateful that education is not his struggle but at the same time, we teach him not settle in life for any reason and every day of his life he should be doing his absolute best!!

Well, as all parents know, yearly they have the "Open House" at the beginning of the school year. This is set up for parents to come in and meet the teacher and look over the curriculum. You get a chance to meet face to face with the teachers. You know, finally put a face with the name and see the learning environment that your kids are in. Most teachers will give the same generic speech. Introduce themselves, why they teach and expectations of the classroom. They go over how they assign work, how often they assign it and when it's due. If you have a real good one, they will give you upcoming projects and due dates as well! I love those!!!

But there is always that time after when the teacher talks to the parent one on one. And year after year, it never fails, we get the same report for my son. The conversation goes a little something like this:

Me: Hi, how are you doing? I'm Corey's father and this is his mother!
Teacher: Really, I'm Mr./Mrs. such and such! Nice to meet you.
Me: Yes, nice to meet you as well!
Teacher: Mmmm hmmm (as they look at my son).
My Wife: Well, we were wondering how he was doing in your class? Is there anything we need to know? Is he giving you problems? How are his grades?
Teacher: Well, he's doing well! I don't really have any problems out of him. He can be a little talkative at times but nothing out of the norm. He's a good kid. And he's really bright!
My Wife: Thank you! How is he doing?

Teacher: Well, right now his grade is a.... But I will tell you this, if he really applied himself he would definitely have an A!!!

Over time, the world has evolved and now we are able to see his grades on the internet throughout the course of the year. For every "B" he brings home, we are able to find a couple of low grades. A week or two when his focus wasn't as strong! Or sometimes there's a test that he didn't study for or a major grade that he didn't take his time with. But whatever the reason is, not having the potential is never the reason. Not being smart enough is not the problem. It is always him not having the mindset to give it everything he has, all the time!

I believe you are "A" material! I believe you have the ability to ace the test of life! I believe that a second-rate life is beneath you! You are better than that! The question is, are you going to give it your all? Are you going to stay focused enough to rise early and go to bed late knowing that your future depends on it? Are you going to give each daily assignment the focus and attention it needs to receive the reward of hard work? You do know hard work pays off? Again, you only get an "A" if you go all the way!!!

Application

1. A normal school year is roughly 39 weeks. Let's make it an even 40 or 10 months. Schedule your life for the next 10 months with daily goals, weekly tests, and major assignments during each month (Please don't be afraid to schedule breaks as well).
2. Find an accountability partner that you can share your plan with to "grade" you on what you turn in as it relates to results.

Chapter 6
Are You Gone Talk or Walk It Out?

In a world where people have declared that conversation rules the nation, the ability to speak is a blessing. God has given us the power to call those things that be not as though they were. You see, we are made in the image of God. And everything that God created, He spoke into existence. God wanted light, so he said let there be light and there was light. God wanted to see trees and plants on the earth, so he said let there be and then there were trees and plants that began to bloom immediately. That same power lies within us. We have the ability to call it like we want it.

Too many times we are speaking from a place of facts and not a place of faith. There is a difference you know. Facts cannot be denied but your faith can change your facts if you apply it correctly. Let me explain. What's in your bank account right now, is really there. The difficulties you are facing right now are really there. That's a fact! But what does your faith say? What does your bank account look like from a place of faith? How bad is your situation when you look at it through the eyes of faith? So many times, I have people tell me they're just a "realist" or they only deal with facts. So, when they speak, they declare what they see. But if you want to see change, you have to declare change! If you are going to speak to your situation, let it be from a place of faith and not facts!

The more you speak positive, the more you'll see positive. You have the ability to set things in motion just by opening your mouth and declaring it. Saying it repeatedly should create the drive for success. Anytime I focus on doing a thing I find myself constantly rehearsing it over and over in my head. Then I will start to say what I want over and over. And somewhere in the midst of saying the thing repeatedly, my drive builds and I find myself moving towards the thing I want to see. **Your confession sparks progression. If you want to move forward, speak forward thoughts.** So, start telling folks how successful you're going to be. Open your mouth and define what success looks like. Let it be known the kind of car you're about to drive!! How big is your house going to be? We will never know until you open your mouth!!

The bible says that death and life are in the power of the tongue and those who love it will eat the fruits of it (Proverbs 18:21). Now fruits are naturally made to give life. They provide the essential vitamins that we need to live a healthy life. My elementary teacher would say that an apple a day, keeps the doctor away! She was trying to teach me that eating my fruits would keep me healthy. And that is so true. But she never considered the fact that the apple could be rotten. And in that case, the very thing that was designed to give me life would be the thing that would send me to the doctor. Ask yourself, how many times have you spoken bad fruit over your life? Because just as speaking positive creates a better life, releasing negative words will create the life you hate. Those words or conversations will leave you stuck in the same position you are in now. Eventually, they will be the reason you find yourself going in a reverse. And who wants to do that? My friends and I growing up would say that we move forward, never backwards as it relates to dating women. It was our way of reminding each other to never go back to a woman we left, because obviously we left them for a reason. I would encourage you to live by the same code. Anytime you feel the urge to go back, remember why that place is behind you. So, start speaking the life you want to live and watch how free you become!

But my question is, are you going to talk or walk it out? In the book of Acts, the 19th chapter, there are many miracles that are spoken of that were worked by the Apostle Paul. Well, the bible tells us that he was casting out spirits and healing people in the name of Jesus. Apparently, the seven sons of Sceva, a high priest, believed they could do it as well. They went to a man that was possessed by an evil spirit and told the spirit to leave in the name of Jesus that Paul talked about. Well, this spirit responded in such a way that left the young men wounded, naked, and running out of the house!

You see if talking was the only thing that we needed to do, then everyone would already have what they needed and wanted. Talking is the beginning but not the end. You need to put a little elbow grease with those words. The seven sons knew how to talk a good game, but were not walking out the lifestyle that allowed that type of power to be revealed. It teaches us all a valuable lesson though.

1. **Your words will expose your lifestyle!**

    The moment you declare a thing, people will begin to look for results. If your walk doesn't match what you are declaring, the results will be detrimental to your health. To speak a thing is to put it in motion. You better make sure your life is in alignment with your dreams and goals before you open your mouth. And then whatever adjustments come with that, be prepared to make them as well. It takes a special type of person to back up what they say.

2. **Your words will trigger the flight or fight response in you!**

    Either you are going to fight for the thing you declared or you will run from it. Not everyone is a fighter but more importantly, not everyone knows how to fight. Knowing how to fight is only half the battle. You must also learn what to fight for. Some things are not worth pursuing. But then there are those things that are essential to life for you. You must learn those things and fight for them the correct way.

3. **Your words can talk you in or out of a home!**

Ever heard the expression that you made your bed so lay in it? Well, your words have the kind of power to create an atmosphere that you will have to live in. If you use the wrong words, that atmosphere can become very chaotic! It makes life very uneasy. It's true that a home is where the heart is, but the heart only wants to live in a place of peace. Depending on how you use those words, you may find yourself out of a home.

So, you see, it's going to take more than words for you to get the manifestation you are waiting on. You are going to have to tighten up your boot straps and put some work in to get this. At this point you have kicked your walls down and created a foundation to build on. You have a plan and instructions! So, what are you waiting for? There's only one thing left to do... walk it out! My Pastor always says that faith has feet. In other words, whatever you are believing for should put you in motion. If you have not moved by now, then it's clear you don't believe. Because when you do, the greater that's on the inside of you will rise up and give you a power that makes you unstoppable!!! You will have no choice but to live free and forever!

Peter found himself in the midst of a storm. With the rain pouring down and the wind blowing uncontrollably, he sees an image of what appears to be Jesus. He asked the simple question, "Lord, if it's you, bid me to come out the box, I mean boat." The bible says that Jesus tells him to come. It is never God's will for you to be stuck in a place and not moving forward. At that moment, Peter makes the decision to move on what God told him to do. He steps out the boat and begins to do the impossible. He walks on water, literally. You see anytime you make the choice to move when you get instructions, you get results that are remarkable. Your fate is inevitable. You position yourself to do the impossible. Even if it's in the worst time of your life. Move when you get the instructions and expect a miracle to happen.

The Apostle James says in his book that we should not just be hearers only, but we need to be doers as well. He states that whoever does that is deceiving himself (James 1:22). Now that's interesting. Most people who "don't do" tend to have the allusion that they are doing what needs to be done. Some are successful and some aren't. But I can guarantee, all of them are unhappy. I personally know people who make over six figures but are still not living a free life. Every last one of them that I have talked to always talks about starting their own business. Some even have a business plan but all of them are stuck in the same place deceiving themselves. They have heard the instructions to a life that will give them the satisfaction that they need but neither one of them have done anything about what they heard. Unfortunately, their present life is being tormented by the life they never lived. **Don't allow your dreams to turn into nightmares that haunt you endlessly.**

Jonah found himself in the same scenario. He had clearly heard from God. He had an assignment and purpose. But for whatever reason, he chose to go a different route and not do what he heard. In fact, God told him to go in one direction, but he chose to go in a totally different direction. To make matters worse, he actually paid a fare to go the wrong way. He then found himself on a boat traveling to where he wanted to go and it was not in the direction of purpose. Then something crazy happened. A great storm broke out. Everyone began praying to their god to try to get an answer of what to do to make it through the storm and to get the storm to cease. They began to throw things off the ship, but it didn't help. Finally, they realized, Jonah was there but he was sleep. So, they woke him up to pray to his God. After they realized he was the reason for the storm, they asked him what he had done. They believed that whatever it was, it caused them all to feel the effects.

Jonah's decision to not walk it out cost him something. He had to pay to go the wrong way. **You need to understand that it costs you to not do what you're supposed to be doing.** Sometimes you pay with sleepless nights. Sometimes you have to give up your peace or your happiness. Is it worth it? I guess living in a box could become comfortable if you let it. Working a 9-5, Monday through Friday, becomes a great means of paying your bills, if you let it. And there's definitely nothing wrong with that, but what happens when working a job gets in the way of destiny? What happens when you look up and ten years later you still have not tapped into what was placed on the inside of you? Sometimes it will cause you to deal with the boss that gets on your nerves day after day after day. You may have to pay the price of frustration and fatigue for the thing that you know was never designed to sustain you. I'm not down playing working for someone else but I want you to know there is a price to be paid for not following the instructions God has given you. And I don't know about you, but at this point, if I'm going to pay a price, at least let it be a down payment on me moving towards destiny and purpose.

Don't forget, the decision you make affects everybody around you. Frustrated people normally create a frantic environment to live in. People who have a hard day at work tend to come home and force their household to have a bad day as well. I remember many days of my personal life making decisions based off of my emotions knowing I could handle the consequences. But then I had to look back and see how it affected my family. The look on my mom's face or the disappointment in my wife's eyes were never worth the storm I forced myself to go through. Not to say that we would not have bad days, but most of it could have been avoided by me doing what I knew was the right thing to do. **Don't force those around you to deal with the storm of your disobedience.**

I want you to imagine the world and the state it's in now. So many people are currently facing life changing decisions in their life. Things are sporadically going wrong and they are in dire need of some answers. They are searching within and even making the decision to get rid of things in their life with the hope of things changing for the better. But no matter how much they try, still the storm is not coming to an end. They are looking for the one with the answers. **The greatest thing you could do for this world is be yourself.** Become everything you were created to be. And in that, there are answers that the world is looking for. The storm did not end until Jonah made the decision to get off the boat first. He would eventually answer the call and many lives were changed for the better.

Floyd Mayweather has made more money from his mouth than he has made from his boxing ability. I watched a documentary on him in which he proclaimed himself to be "Boxing's Bad Boy"! There was a time in his life when he was pushing to make it to the top. He was stuck in a place that was far too small for him. There was something in him that said that greater was there and he needed to strive to reach another level if he really wanted to live his dreams. And before long, he needed to put his faith in action!

He started boxing at a young age. He came from a family of fighters and though he had the boxing skills, at one point in his life, he needed to fire his father. He loved his father, but he did not have what it took to get him to the next level. His current management team believed in him but not enough to put him up for the major title fights. They believed that Oscar De La Hoya would be a bigger payout due to the Hispanic community spending more money on Pay Per View. So, he took his own money and created Mayweather's Promotions. He then signed himself to his company and began to promote his own fights. The next step was to create a team, "The Money Team" he called it. This meant he had to change some of his circle to better position himself for where he was going.

With the team in place, and doing his own promotion, he needed a strategy that was out the box. That's when he realized the boxing world needed a villain. Before every fight there is a promotion phase. This is when the two fighters tour the country to make sure people become interested in watching the fight. So he would make statements like, "I'm running my mouth a lot and I'm looking for a guy to shut me up. If you don't shut me up, I'm going to keep running my mouth." Or allow his ego to go haywire and say things like, "You have to realize that most of these guys get in there and fight with heart. I fight with smarts. There is no fighter that is smarter than me. Most of these fighters are ABC, 1-2-3. I am like 4-5-6 levels above them; that's why I'm able to beat them." When asked about Manny Pacquiao he said, "There is boxing and then there is me. The rest are just falling in line behind me or are trying to get in line to fight me. And that includes Manny Pacquiao too." You see Floyd gained the understanding that whether you hated or loved him, you would pay to see him fight with the anticipation of seeing him either lose or win. And that was a win/win scenario for him.

He made every effort to become the man people either loved or hated. Despite what most people said about his character, he stuck with it. Contrary to all the critics, he went all the way with his plan. On May 2, 2015, Mayweather defeated Pacquiao in what was deemed to be the "fight of the century" to unify the welterweight titles of the world. In that one fight, it is speculated that he made over 300 million. He received 100 of that before the fight. He made 25 million off of endorsements for the fight and the Pay Per View numbers were outrageous. This was by far the most lucrative boxing match in history. To put this in perspective, this one fight made him more money than Tim Duncan made over an 18-year career and he is a 5-time World Champion, 2-time NBA MVP, 3 times finals MVP and was named the Rookie of the Year. In that one year, he made more money than any other sports athlete ever made surpassing names like Michael Jordan and Tiger Woods.

What made him successful? He not only talked a good game, but he backed it up. As of now, he is only the second person in boxing history to become 49-0. You can say what you want about the man, may not like his antics, ego or fighting style, but you have to respect the business man that he became. The courage and faith he displayed to step out of the box and do what has never been done to get what he always knew he could have. Against all odds he has made his mark in history. For generations to come, you will not be able to mention boxing without mentioning Floyd Mayweather, no matter what the connotation is.

So, what's it gone be? By now you should be claustrophobic! The idea of a box should make you sick to your stomach. But the good thing is, you are better positioned today than you were yesterday. You know exactly what it is that you want and need to do and you have a plan in place. Now is the time to step out on faith. Every action from this point needs to be a step forward. No more standing still or being complacent on the gift you have to offer the world. You are now ready to come of the box...Live free and forever!

I pray that one day, I will make my mark in history. It has always been a passion of mine to leave behind a name that speaks to all generations. A legacy that my family can be proud of!! But even more than that, I want to be the guy that helped others reach their full potential. This book was written to help others live life outside the box. And though we may never meet face to face, may this book be the launching pad for your success!!! Go live life out of the box!!! LIVE FREE AND FOREVER!!!